The Organized Blogger

Twelve Monthly Sections to Plan Out Your Blog Material

Let's Get Started...

BLOG TITLE:

DOMAIN:

TARGET AUDIENCE:

NICHE OVERVIEW:

MAIN FOCUS:

PRIMARY KEYWORDS:

MAIN TRAFFIC SOURCES:

Blog Management

ADMIN LOGIN INFORMATION:

AFFILIATE ACCOUNTS:

ADVERTISER ACCOUNTS:

HOSTING ACCOUNT LOGIN:

Important Contacts

PARTNERS:

OTHER:

Social Media

TWITTER

@_____

FACEBOOK

INSTAGRAM

@_____

PINTEREST

OTHER

OTHER

OTHER

OTHER

Brand Creation

SLOGAN / TAGLINE:

WRITING & CONTENT STYLE:

NICHE SUMMARY:

6 WORDS TO DESCRIBE MY BLOG:

HOW MY BLOG PROVIDES VALUE:

MISSION STATEMENT:

Blog Design

BLOG STYLE OBJECTIVE:

PRIMARY FONTS USED:

COLOR SCHEME:

THEME USED:

LOGO / GRAPHIC DESIGNER:

DESIGN CHECKLIST:

Verify responsive design

Create 404 landing page

Install contact form & opt in

Create advertiser side widgets

Test links in navigation menu

Install Cookie Permission Plugin

Install Privacy Agreement

PLUGIN CHECKLIST:

Install SEO plugin

Install WP Total Cache

Install social sharing plugin

Install WP Forms

Install Google Analytics

Install Backup Plugin

Install Opt-in Plugin

Affiliate Accounts

ADVERTISER ACCOUNTS: AFFILIATE ACCOUNTS:

Marketing Planner

TOP TRAFFIC CHANNELS:

MARKETING TO DO LIST:

FREE ADVERTISING IDEAS:

PAID ADVERTISING IDEAS:

Notes

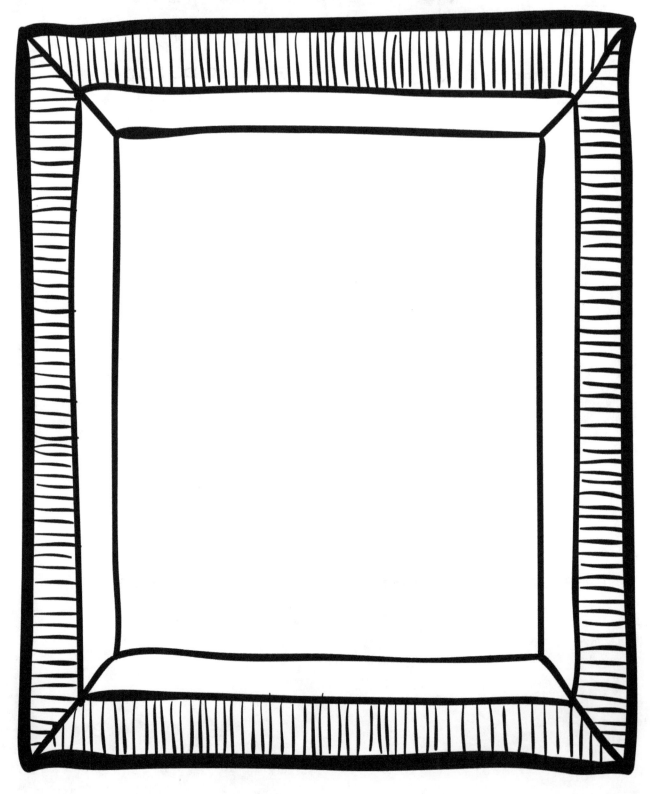

Notes

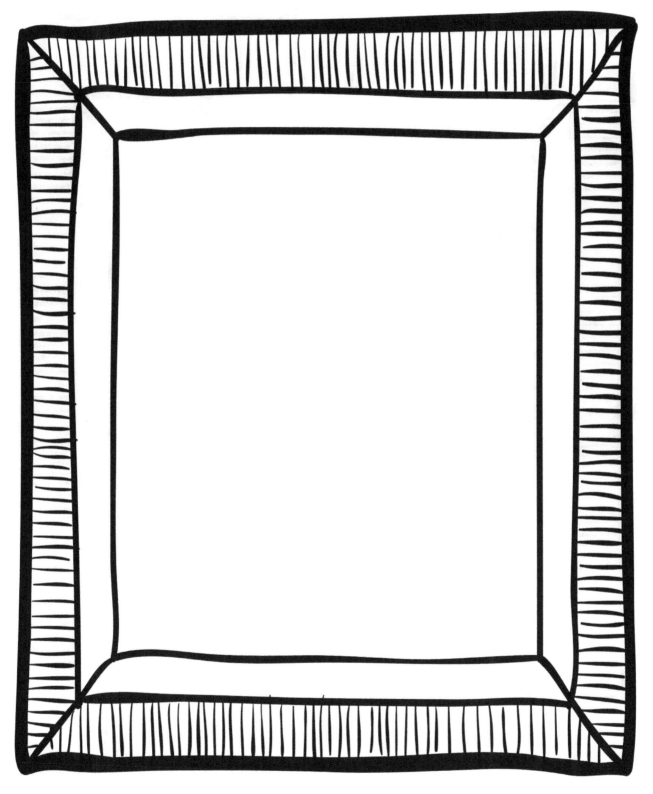

Notes

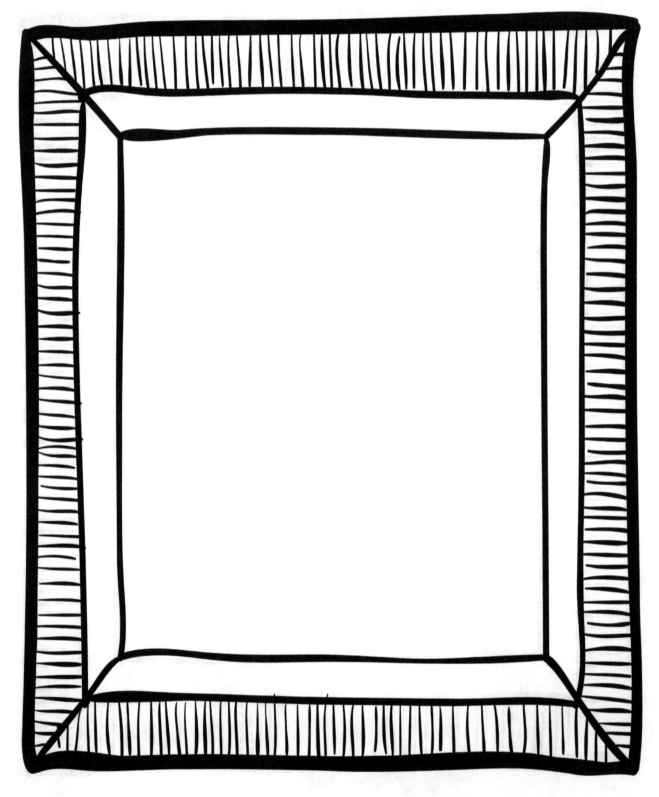

Notes

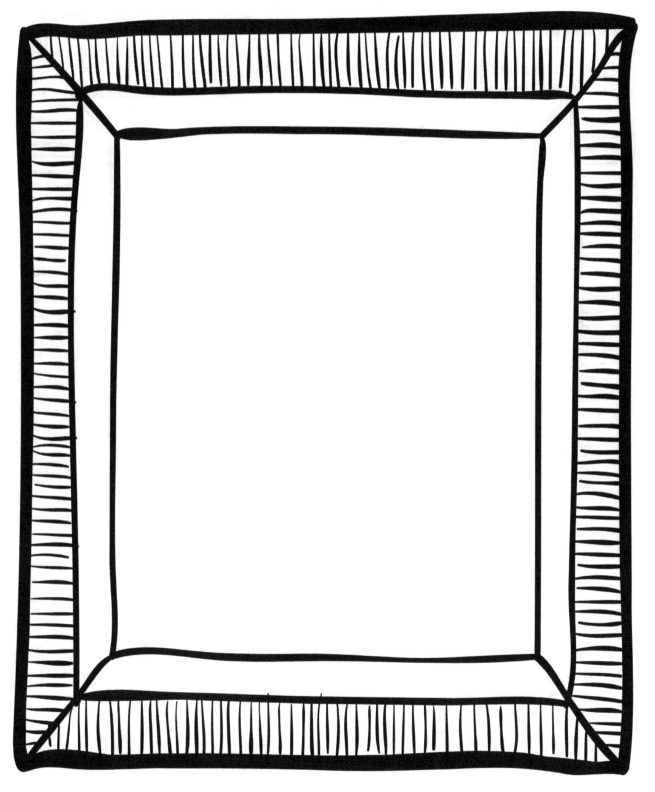

Notes

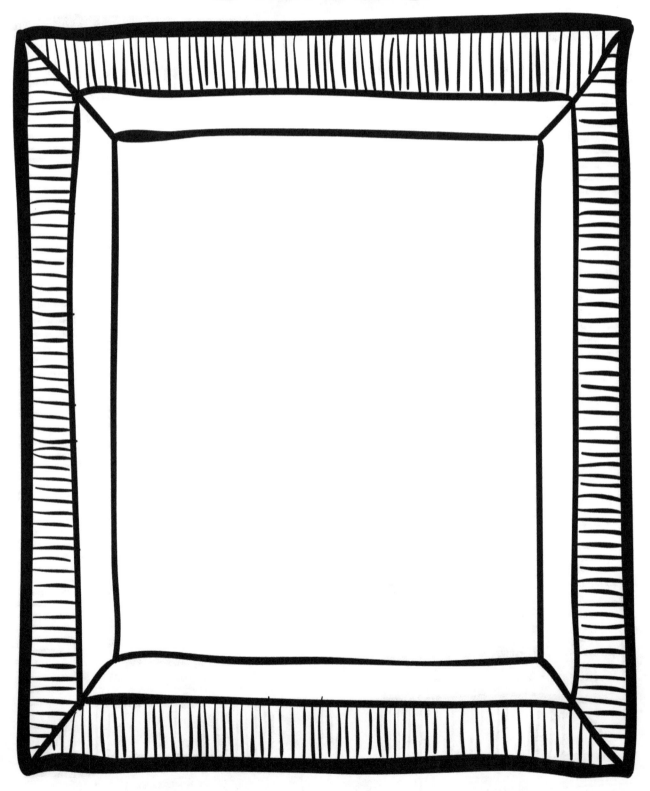

January

TASKS, MARKETING, ENGAGEMENT & MONETIZATION

CONTENT IDEAS

PROMOTION IDEAS

TOP PRIORITIES

MONTHLY FOCUS

MONETIZATION IDEAS

Monthly Goals

MAIN OBJECTIVE:

GOAL:

ACTION STEPS:

GOAL:

ACTION STEPS:

GOAL:

ACTION STEPS:

TRAFFIC STATS:

MAILING LIST SUBSCRIBERS:

Content Planner

POST TITLE:

PUBLICATION DATE:

TARGETED KEYWORDS:

TO DO CHECKLIST:

- Research Topic
- Pinpoint Target Audience
- Choose target keywords
- Optimize for search engines
- Link to other blog post
- Create post images
- Proofread & Edit Post
- Schedule Post Date

SOCIAL SHARING:

TOPIC OUTLINE:

NOTES:

Content Planner

CATEGORY:

RESOURCE LINKS:

SEO CHECKLIST:

- Primary keyword in post title

- Secondary keyword in sub-title

- Keyword in first paragraph

- Word count > 1000 words

- 1-2 Outbound Links

- Internal Link Structure

- Post URL includes keywords

- Meta description added

- Post includes images

- Post includes sub-headlines

- Social sharing enabled

GRAPHICS/IMAGES:

KEY POINTS:

NOTES:

Post Planner

WEEK OF: _____

TYPE: ARTICLE: ☐   TUTORIAL: ☐   REVIEW: ☐   GUEST POST: ☐

PUBLICATION DATE:

TITLE:

CATEGORY:

KEYWORDS:

NOTES:

PUBLICATION DATE:

TITLE:

CATEGORY:

KEYWORDS:

NOTES:

PUBLICATION DATE:

TITLE:

CATEGORY:

KEYWORDS:

NOTES:

Post Planner

WEEK OF: _____

TYPE: ARTICLE: ☐   TUTORIAL: ☐   REVIEW: ☐   GUEST POST: ☐

PUBLICATION DATE:

TITLE:

CATEGORY:

KEYWORDS:

NOTES:

PUBLICATION DATE:

TITLE:

CATEGORY:

KEYWORDS:

NOTES:

PUBLICATION DATE:

TITLE:

CATEGORY:

KEYWORDS:

NOTES:

Post Planner

WEEK OF: _____

TYPE: ARTICLE ☐   TUTORIAL: ☐   REVIEW: ☐   GUEST POST: ☐

PUBLICATION DATE:

TITLE:

CATEGORY:

KEYWORDS:

NOTES:

LIST BUILDING PROGRESS:

SUBSCRIBERS: _____   EMAILED THIS WEEK ✉

SOCIAL MEDIA PROMO THIS WEEK:

☐ 🐦   ☐ f   ☐ 𝓅   ☐ 📷   ☐ ▶   ☐ in   ☐ g+

EXTERNAL LINKS: PRODUCTS PROMOTED:

INTERNAL LINKS:

                                         Affiliate Disclaimer
                                         Included

Guest Post Planner

POST TITLE:

PUBLISH DATE: CATEGORY:

MAIN TOPIC:

POST SUMMARY:

KEY POINTS:

INCLUDED LINKS: SHARED ON: FACEBOOK   INSTAGRAM

                                       TWITTER   PINTEREST

TAGS & KEYWORDS: # OF COMMENTS: # OF TRACKBACKS:

                                  NOTES:

Marketing Planner

TOP TRAFFIC CHANNELS:

MARKETING TO DO LIST:

FREE ADVERTISING IDEAS:

PAID ADVERTISING IDEAS:

Marketing Tracker

PROMOTIONAL STRATEGIES TO MAXIMIZE EXPOSURE

PROMOTIONAL IDEAS:

MARKETING TO DO:

SOCIAL MEDIA GROWTH TRACKER:

BEFORE: AFTER:

OTHER:

LIST BUILDING & ENGAGEMENT:

MAILING LIST
SUBSCRIBERS:

OF EMAILS SENT
TO SUBSCRIBERS:

OF NEW BLOG
POSTS THIS WEEK:

OF COMPLETED
GUEST POSTS:

NOTES:

February

TASKS, MARKETING, ENGAGEMENT & MONETIZATION

CONTENT IDEAS

PROMOTION IDEAS

TOP PRIORITIES

MONTHLY FOCUS

MONETIZATION RESOURCES

Monthly Goals

MAIN OBJECTIVE:

GOAL:

ACTION STEPS:

GOAL:

ACTION STEPS:

GOAL:

ACTION STEPS:

TRAFFIC STATS:

MAILING LIST SUBSCRIBERS:

Content Planner

POST TITLE:

TARGETED KEYWORDS:

PUBLICATION DATE:

TO DO CHECKLIST:

Research Topic

Pinpoint Target Audience

Choose target keywords

Optimize for search engines

Link to other blog post

Create post images

Proofread & Edit Post

Schedule Post Date

NOTES:

SOCIAL SHARING:

TOPIC OUTLINE:

Content Planner

CATEGORY:

RESOURCE LINKS:

GRAPHICS/IMAGES:

KEY POINTS:

SEO CHECKLIST:

Primary keyword in post title

Secondary keyword in sub-title

Keyword in first paragraph

Word count > 1000 words

1-2 Outbound Links

Internal Link Structure

Post URL includes keywords

Meta description added

Post includes images

Post includes sub-headlines

Social sharing enabled

NOTES:

Post Planner

WEEK OF: _____

TYPE: ARTICLE: ☐   TUTORIAL: ☐   REVIEW: ☐   GUEST POST: ☐

PUBLICATION DATE:

TITLE:

CATEGORY:

KEYWORDS:

NOTES:

PUBLICATION DATE:

TITLE:

CATEGORY:

KEYWORDS:

NOTES:

PUBLICATION DATE:

TITLE:

CATEGORY:

KEYWORDS:

NOTES:

Post Planner

WEEK OF: _____

TYPE: ARTICLE: TUTORIAL: REVIEW: GUEST POST:

PUBLICATION DATE:

TITLE:

CATEGORY:

KEYWORDS:

NOTES:

PUBLICATION DATE:

TITLE:

CATEGORY:

KEYWORDS:

NOTES:

PUBLICATION DATE:

TITLE:

CATEGORY:

KEYWORDS:

NOTES:

Post Planner

WEEK OF: _____

TYPE: ARTICLE: TUTORIAL: REVIEW: GUEST POST:

PUBLICATION DATE:

TITLE:

CATEGORY:

KEYWORDS:

NOTES:

LIST BUILDING PROGRESS:

SUBSCRIBERS: EMAILED THIS WEEK ✉

SOCIAL MEDIA PROMO THIS WEEK:

☐ 🐦   ☐ f   ☐ P   ☐ 📷   ☐ ▶   in   g+

EXTERNAL LINKS: PRODUCTS PROMOTED:

INTERNAL LINKS:

Affiliate Disclaimer
Included

Guest Post Planner

POST TITLE:

PUBLISH DATE: CATEGORY:

MAIN TOPIC:

POST SUMMARY:

KEY POINTS:

INCLUDED LINKS:

SHARED ON:

FACEBOOK   INSTAGRAM

TWITTER   PINTEREST

TAGS & KEYWORDS:

OF COMMENTS: # OF TRACKBACKS:

NOTES:

Marketing Planner

TOP TRAFFIC CHANNELS:

MARKETING TO DO LIST:

FREE ADVERTISING IDEAS:

PAID ADVERTISING IDEAS:

Marketing Tracker

PROMOTIONAL STRATEGIES TO MAXIMIZE EXPOSURE

PROMOTIONAL IDEAS:

MARKETING TO DO:

SOCIAL MEDIA GROWTH TRACKER:

BEFORE: AFTER:

OTHER:

LIST BUILDING & ENGAGEMENT:

MAILING LIST
SUBSCRIBERS:

OF EMAILS SENT
TO SUBSCRIBERS:

OF NEW BLOG
POSTS THIS WEEK:

OF COMPLETED
GUEST POSTS:

NOTES:

March

TASKS, MARKETING, ENGAGEMENT & MONETIZATION

CONTENT IDEAS

PROMOTION IDEAS

TOP PRIORITIES

MONTHLY FOCUS

MONETIZATION RESOURCES

Monthly Goals

MAIN OBJECTIVE:

GOAL:

ACTION STEPS:

GOAL:

ACTION STEPS:

GOAL:

ACTION STEPS:

TRAFFIC STATS:

MAILING LIST SUBSCRIBERS:

Content Planner

POST TITLE:

PUBLICATION DATE:

TARGETED KEYWORDS:

TO DO CHECKLIST:

Research Topic

Pinpoint Target Audience

Choose target keywords

Optimize for search engines

Link to other blog post

Create post images

Proofread & Edit Post

Schedule Post Date

SOCIAL SHARING:

TOPIC OUTLINE:

NOTES:

Content Planner

CATEGORY:

RESOURCE LINKS:

GRAPHICS/IMAGES:

KEY POINTS:

SEO CHECKLIST:

Primary keyword in post title

Secondary keyword in sub-title

Keyword in first paragraph

Word count > 1000 words

1-2 Outbound Links

Internal Link Structure

Post URL includes keywords

Meta description added

Post includes images

Post includes sub-headlines

Social sharing enabled

NOTES:

Post Planner

WEEK OF: _____

TYPE: ARTICLE   TUTORIAL: REVIEW: GUEST POST:

PUBLICATION DATE:

TITLE:

CATEGORY:

KEYWORDS:

NOTES:

PUBLICATION DATE:

TITLE:

CATEGORY:

KEYWORDS:

NOTES:

PUBLICATION DATE:

TITLE:

CATEGORY:

KEYWORDS:

NOTES:

Post Planner

WEEK OF: _____

TYPE: ARTICLE ☐   TUTORIAL: ☐   REVIEW: ☐   GUEST POST: ☐

PUBLICATION DATE:

TITLE:

CATEGORY:

KEYWORDS:

NOTES:

PUBLICATION DATE:

TITLE:

CATEGORY:

KEYWORDS:

NOTES:

PUBLICATION DATE:

TITLE:

CATEGORY:

KEYWORDS:

NOTES:

Post Planner

WEEK OF: _____

TYPE: ARTICLE: ☐   TUTORIAL: ☐   REVIEW: ☐   GUEST POST: ☐

PUBLICATION DATE:

TITLE:

CATEGORY:

KEYWORDS:

NOTES:

LIST BUILDING PROGRESS:

SUBSCRIBERS: EMAILED THIS WEEK ✉

SOCIAL MEDIA PROMO THIS WEEK:

☐ 🐦   ☐ f   ☐ 🅿   ☐ 📷   ☐ ▶   ☐ in   g+

EXTERNAL LINKS: PRODUCTS PROMOTED:

INTERNAL LINKS:

Affiliate Disclaimer
Included

Guest Post Planner

POST TITLE:

PUBLISH DATE: CATEGORY:

MAIN TOPIC:

POST SUMMARY:

KEY POINTS:

INCLUDED LINKS:

SHARED ON:

FACEBOOK   INSTAGRAM

TWITTER   PINTEREST

TAGS & KEYWORDS:

OF COMMENTS: # OF TRACKBACKS:

NOTES:

Marketing Planner

TOP TRAFFIC CHANNELS:

MARKETING TO DO LIST:

FREE ADVERTISING IDEAS:

PAID ADVERTISING IDEAS:

Marketing Tracker

PROMOTIONAL STRATEGIES TO MAXIMIZE EXPOSURE

PROMOTIONAL IDEAS:

MARKETING TO DO:

SOCIAL MEDIA GROWTH TRACKER:

	BEFORE:	AFTER:
f		
P		

OTHER:

LIST BUILDING & ENGAGEMENT:

MAILING LIST SUBSCRIBERS:	
# OF EMAILS SENT TO SUBSCRIBERS:	
# OF NEW BLOG POSTS THIS WEEK:	
# OF COMPLETED GUEST POSTS:	

NOTES:

April

TASKS, MARKETING, ENGAGEMENT & MONETIZATION

CONTENT IDEAS

PROMOTION IDEAS

TOP PRIORITIES

MONTHLY FOCUS

MONETIZATION RESOURCES

Monthly Goals

MAIN OBJECTIVE:

GOAL:

ACTION STEPS:

GOAL:

ACTION STEPS:

GOAL:

ACTION STEPS:

TRAFFIC STATS:

MAILING LIST SUBSCRIBERS:

Content Planner

POST TITLE:

PUBLICATION DATE:

TARGETED KEYWORDS:

TO DO CHECKLIST:

Research Topic

Pinpoint Target Audience

Choose target keywords

Optimize for search engines

SOCIAL SHARING:

Link to other blog post

Create post images

Proofread & Edit Post

TOPIC OUTLINE:

Schedule Post Date

NOTES:

Content Planner

CATEGORY:

RESOURCE LINKS:

GRAPHICS/IMAGES:

KEY POINTS:

SEO CHECKLIST:

- Primary keyword in post title
- Secondary keyword in sub-title
- Keyword in first paragraph
- Word count > 1000 words
- 1-2 Outbound Links
- Internal Link Structure
- Post URL includes keywords
- Meta description added
- Post includes images
- Post includes sub-headlines
- Social sharing enabled

NOTES:

Post Planner

WEEK OF: _____

TYPE: ARTICLE: ☐ TUTORIAL: ☐ REVIEW: ☐ GUEST POST: ☐

PUBLICATION DATE:

TITLE:

CATEGORY:

KEYWORDS:

NOTES:

PUBLICATION DATE:

TITLE:

CATEGORY:

KEYWORDS:

NOTES:

PUBLICATION DATE:

TITLE:

CATEGORY:

KEYWORDS:

NOTES:

Post Planner

WEEK OF: _____

TYPE: ARTICLE: TUTORIAL: REVIEW: GUEST POST:

PUBLICATION DATE:

TITLE:

CATEGORY:

KEYWORDS:

NOTES:

PUBLICATION DATE:

TITLE:

CATEGORY:

KEYWORDS:

NOTES:

PUBLICATION DATE:

TITLE:

CATEGORY:

KEYWORDS:

NOTES:

Post Planner

WEEK OF: _____

TYPE: ARTICLE: TUTORIAL: REVIEW: GUEST POST:

PUBLICATION DATE:

TITLE:

CATEGORY:

KEYWORDS:

NOTES:

LIST BUILDING PROGRESS:

SUBSCRIBERS: EMAILED THIS WEEK

SOCIAL MEDIA PROMO THIS WEEK:

EXTERNAL LINKS: PRODUCTS PROMOTED:

INTERNAL LINKS:

Affiliate Disclaimer
Included

Guest Post Planner

POST TITLE:

PUBLISH DATE: CATEGORY:

MAIN TOPIC:

POST SUMMARY:

KEY POINTS:

INCLUDED LINKS:

SHARED ON:

FACEBOOK   INSTAGRAM

TWITTER   PINTEREST

TAGS & KEYWORDS:

OF COMMENTS: # OF TRACKBACKS:

NOTES:

Marketing Planner

TOP TRAFFIC CHANNELS:

MARKETING TO DO LIST:

FREE ADVERTISING IDEAS:

PAID ADVERTISING IDEAS:

Marketing Tracker

PROMOTIONAL STRATEGIES TO MAXIMIZE EXPOSURE

PROMOTIONAL IDEAS:

MARKETING TO DO:

SOCIAL MEDIA GROWTH TRACKER:

BEFORE: AFTER:

f

Instagram

Twitter

P

YouTube

OTHER:

LIST BUILDING & ENGAGEMENT:

MAILING LIST
SUBSCRIBERS:

OF EMAILS SENT
TO SUBSCRIBERS:

OF NEW BLOG
POSTS THIS WEEK:

OF COMPLETED
GUEST POSTS:

NOTES:

May

TASKS, MARKETING, ENGAGEMENT & MONETIZATION

CONTENT IDEAS

PROMOTION IDEAS

TOP PRIORITIES

MONTHLY FOCUS

MONETIZATION RESOURCES

Monthly Goals

MAIN OBJECTIVE:

GOAL:

ACTION STEPS:

GOAL:

ACTION STEPS:

GOAL:

ACTION STEPS:

TRAFFIC STATS:

MAILING LIST SUBSCRIBERS:

Content Planner

POST TITLE:

PUBLICATION DATE:

TARGETED KEYWORDS:

TO DO CHECKLIST:

- Research Topic
- Pinpoint Target Audience
- Choose target keywords
- Optimize for search engines
- Link to other blog post
- Create post images
- Proofread & Edit Post
- Schedule Post Date

SOCIAL SHARING:

TOPIC OUTLINE:

NOTES:

Content Planner

CATEGORY:

RESOURCE LINKS:

GRAPHICS/IMAGES:

KEY POINTS:

SEO CHECKLIST:

- Primary keyword in post title
- Secondary keyword in sub-title
- Keyword in first paragraph
- Word count > 1000 words
- 1-2 Outbound Links
- Internal Link Structure
- Post URL includes keywords
- Meta description added
- Post includes images
- Post includes sub-headlines
- Social sharing enabled

NOTES:

Post Planner

WEEK OF: _____

TYPE: ARTICLE: ☐   TUTORIAL: ☐   REVIEW: ☐   GUEST POST: ☐

PUBLICATION DATE:

TITLE:

CATEGORY:

KEYWORDS:

NOTES:

PUBLICATION DATE:

TITLE:

CATEGORY:

KEYWORDS:

NOTES:

PUBLICATION DATE:

TITLE:

CATEGORY:

KEYWORDS:

NOTES:

Post Planner

WEEK OF: _____

TYPE: ARTICLE: ☐   TUTORIAL: ☐   REVIEW: ☐   GUEST POST: ☐

PUBLICATION DATE:

TITLE:

CATEGORY:

KEYWORDS:

NOTES:

PUBLICATION DATE:

TITLE:

CATEGORY:

KEYWORDS:

NOTES:

PUBLICATION DATE:

TITLE:

CATEGORY:

KEYWORDS:

NOTES:

Post Planner

WEEK OF: _____

TYPE: ARTICLE: ☐   TUTORIAL: ☐   REVIEW: ☐   GUEST POST: ☐

PUBLICATION DATE:

TITLE:

CATEGORY:

KEYWORDS:

NOTES:

LIST BUILDING PROGRESS:

SUBSCRIBERS: _____   EMAILED THIS WEEK ✉

SOCIAL MEDIA PROMO THIS WEEK:

☐ 🐦   ☐ f   ☐ 📌   ☐ 📷   ☐ ▶   ☐ in   ☐ g+

EXTERNAL LINKS: PRODUCTS PROMOTED:

INTERNAL LINKS:

Affiliate Disclaimer
Included

Guest Post Planner

POST TITLE:

PUBLISH DATE: CATEGORY:

MAIN TOPIC:

POST SUMMARY:

KEY POINTS:

INCLUDED LINKS:

SHARED ON:
FACEBOOK   INSTAGRAM

TWITTER   PINTEREST

TAGS & KEYWORDS:

OF COMMENTS: # OF TRACKBACKS:

NOTES:

Marketing Planner

TOP TRAFFIC CHANNELS:

MARKETING TO DO LIST:

FREE ADVERTISING IDEAS:

PAID ADVERTISING IDEAS:

Marketing Tracker

PROMOTIONAL STRATEGIES TO MAXIMIZE EXPOSURE

PROMOTIONAL IDEAS:

MARKETING TO DO:

SOCIAL MEDIA GROWTH TRACKER:

BEFORE: AFTER:

f

(Instagram)

(Twitter)

P

(YouTube)

OTHER:

LIST BUILDING & ENGAGEMENT:

MAILING LIST SUBSCRIBERS:

 # OF EMAILS SENT TO SUBSCRIBERS:

 # OF NEW BLOG POSTS THIS WEEK:

 # OF COMPLETED GUEST POSTS:

NOTES:

JUNE

CONTENT IDEAS

PROMOTION IDEAS

TOP PRIORITIES

MONTHLY FOCUS

MONETIZATION RESOURCES

Monthly Goals

MAIN OBJECTIVE:

GOAL:

ACTION STEPS:

GOAL:

ACTION STEPS:

GOAL:

ACTION STEPS:

TRAFFIC STATS:

MAILING LIST SUBSCRIBERS:

Content Planner

POST TITLE:

PUBLICATION DATE:

TARGETED KEYWORDS:

TO DO CHECKLIST:

Research Topic

Pinpoint Target Audience

Choose target keywords

Optimize for search engines

Link to other blog post

SOCIAL SHARING:

Create post images

Proofread & Edit Post

Schedule Post Date

TOPIC OUTLINE:

NOTES:

Content Planner

CATEGORY:

SEO CHECKLIST:

RESOURCE LINKS:

Primary keyword in post title

Secondary keyword in sub-title

Keyword in first paragraph

Word count > 1000 words

1-2 Outbound Links

GRAPHICS/IMAGES:

Internal Link Structure

Post URL includes keywords

Meta description added

KEY POINTS:

Post includes images

Post includes sub-headlines

Social sharing enabled

NOTES:

Post Planner

WEEK OF: _____

TYPE: ARTICLE: ☐ TUTORIAL: ☐ REVIEW: ☐ GUEST POST: ☐

PUBLICATION DATE:

TITLE:

CATEGORY:

KEYWORDS:

NOTES:

PUBLICATION DATE:

TITLE:

CATEGORY:

KEYWORDS:

NOTES:

PUBLICATION DATE:

TITLE:

CATEGORY:

KEYWORDS:

NOTES:

Post Planner

WEEK OF: _____

TYPE: ARTICLE: ☐   TUTORIAL: ☐   REVIEW: ☐   GUEST POST: ☐

PUBLICATION DATE:

TITLE:

CATEGORY:

KEYWORDS:

NOTES:

PUBLICATION DATE:

TITLE:

CATEGORY:

KEYWORDS:

NOTES:

PUBLICATION DATE:

TITLE:

CATEGORY:

KEYWORDS:

NOTES:

Post Planner

WEEK OF: _____

TYPE: ARTICLE: ☐   TUTORIAL: ☐   REVIEW: ☐   GUEST POST: ☐

PUBLICATION DATE:

TITLE:

CATEGORY:

KEYWORDS:

NOTES:

LIST BUILDING PROGRESS:

SUBSCRIBERS: _____   EMAILED THIS WEEK ✉

SOCIAL MEDIA PROMO THIS WEEK:

☐ 🐦 ☐ f ☐ 📌 ☐ 📷 ☐ ▶ in g+

EXTERNAL LINKS: PRODUCTS PROMOTED:

INTERNAL LINKS:

Affiliate Disclaimer
Included

Guest Post Planner

POST TITLE:

PUBLISH DATE: CATEGORY:

MAIN TOPIC:

POST SUMMARY:

KEY POINTS:

INCLUDED LINKS: SHARED ON: FACEBOOK   INSTAGRAM

                                       TWITTER   PINTEREST

TAGS & KEYWORDS: # OF COMMENTS: # OF TRACKBACKS:

                             NOTES:

Marketing Planner

TOP TRAFFIC CHANNELS:

MARKETING TO DO LIST:

FREE ADVERTISING IDEAS:

PAID ADVERTISING IDEAS:

Marketing Tracker

PROMOTIONAL STRATEGIES TO MAXIMIZE EXPOSURE

PROMOTIONAL IDEAS:

MARKETING TO DO:

SOCIAL MEDIA GROWTH TRACKER:

	BEFORE:	AFTER:
f		
(Instagram)		
(Twitter)		
(Pinterest)		
(YouTube)		

OTHER:

LIST BUILDING & ENGAGEMENT:

MAILING LIST SUBSCRIBERS:

 # OF EMAILS SENT TO SUBSCRIBERS:

 # OF NEW BLOG POSTS THIS WEEK:

 # OF COMPLETED GUEST POSTS:

NOTES:

JULY

TASKS, MARKETING, ENGAGEMENT & MONETIZATION

CONTENT IDEAS

PROMOTION IDEAS

TOP PRIORITIES

MONTHLY FOCUS

MONETIZATION RESOURCES

Monthly Goals

MAIN OBJECTIVE:

GOAL:

ACTION STEPS:

GOAL:

ACTION STEPS:

GOAL:

ACTION STEPS:

TRAFFIC STATS:

MAILING LIST SUBSCRIBERS:

Content Planner

POST TITLE:

PUBLICATION DATE:

TARGETED KEYWORDS:

TO DO CHECKLIST:

Research Topic

Pinpoint Target Audience

Choose target keywords

Optimize for search engines

Link to other blog post

Create post images

Proofread & Edit Post

Schedule Post Date

SOCIAL SHARING:

TOPIC OUTLINE:

NOTES:

Content Planner

CATEGORY:

RESOURCE LINKS:

GRAPHICS/IMAGES:

KEY POINTS:

SEO CHECKLIST:

Primary keyword in post title

Secondary keyword in sub-title

Keyword in first paragraph

Word count > 1000 words

1-2 Outbound Links

Internal Link Structure

Post URL includes keywords

Meta description added

Post includes images

Post includes sub-headlines

Social sharing enabled

NOTES:

Post Planner

WEEK OF: _____

TYPE: ARTICLE: TUTORIAL: REVIEW: GUEST POST:

PUBLICATION DATE:

TITLE:

CATEGORY:

KEYWORDS:

NOTES:

PUBLICATION DATE:

TITLE:

CATEGORY:

KEYWORDS:

NOTES:

PUBLICATION DATE:

TITLE:

CATEGORY:

KEYWORDS:

NOTES:

Post Planner

WEEK OF: _____

TYPE: ARTICLE: ☐   TUTORIAL: ☐   REVIEW: ☐   GUEST POST: ☐

PUBLICATION DATE:

TITLE:

CATEGORY:

KEYWORDS:

NOTES:

PUBLICATION DATE:

TITLE:

CATEGORY:

KEYWORDS:

NOTES:

PUBLICATION DATE:

TITLE:

CATEGORY:

KEYWORDS:

NOTES:

Post Planner

WEEK OF: _____

TYPE: ARTICLE: ☐   TUTORIAL: ☐   REVIEW: ☐   GUEST POST: ☐

PUBLICATION DATE:

TITLE:

CATEGORY:

KEYWORDS:

NOTES:

LIST BUILDING PROGRESS:

SUBSCRIBERS: EMAILED THIS WEEK ✉

SOCIAL MEDIA PROMO THIS WEEK:

☐ 🐦   ☐ f   ☐ 📌   ☐ 📷   ☐ ▶   in   g+

EXTERNAL LINKS: PRODUCTS PROMOTED:

INTERNAL LINKS:

Affiliate Disclaimer
Included

Guest Post Planner

POST TITLE:

PUBLISH DATE: CATEGORY:

MAIN TOPIC:

POST SUMMARY:

KEY POINTS:

INCLUDED LINKS:

SHARED ON:

FACEBOOK   INSTAGRAM

TWITTER   PINTEREST

TAGS & KEYWORDS:

OF COMMENTS: # OF TRACKBACKS:

NOTES:

Marketing Planner

TOP TRAFFIC CHANNELS:

MARKETING TO DO LIST:

FREE ADVERTISING IDEAS:

PAID ADVERTISING IDEAS:

Marketing Tracker

PROMOTIONAL IDEAS:

MARKETING TO DO:

SOCIAL MEDIA GROWTH TRACKER:

BEFORE: AFTER:

f

◎

🐦

𝓟

▶

OTHER:

LIST BUILDING & ENGAGEMENT:

MAILING LIST
SUBSCRIBERS:

OF EMAILS SENT
TO SUBSCRIBERS:

OF NEW BLOG
POSTS THIS WEEK:

OF COMPLETED
GUEST POSTS:

NOTES:

August

TASKS, MARKETING, ENGAGEMENT & MONETIZATION

CONTENT IDEAS

PROMOTION IDEAS

TOP PRIORITIES

MONTHLY FOCUS

MONETIZATION RESOURCES

Monthly Goals

MAIN OBJECTIVE:

GOAL:

ACTION STEPS:

GOAL:

ACTION STEPS:

GOAL:

ACTION STEPS:

TRAFFIC STATS:

MAILING LIST SUBSCRIBERS:

Content Planner

POST TITLE:

PUBLICATION DATE:

TARGETED KEYWORDS:

TO DO CHECKLIST:

Research Topic

Pinpoint Target Audience

Choose target keywords

Optimize for search engines

SOCIAL SHARING:

Link to other blog post

Create post images

Proofread & Edit Post

TOPIC OUTLINE:

Schedule Post Date

NOTES:

Content Planner

CATEGORY:

RESOURCE LINKS:

GRAPHICS/IMAGES:

KEY POINTS:

SEO CHECKLIST:

- Primary keyword in post title
- Secondary keyword in sub-title
- Keyword in first paragraph
- Word count > 1000 words
- 1-2 Outbound Links
- Internal Link Structure
- Post URL includes keywords
- Meta description added
- Post includes images
- Post includes sub-headlines
- Social sharing enabled

NOTES:

Post Planner

WEEK OF: _____

TYPE: ARTICLE: ☐   TUTORIAL: ☐   REVIEW: ☐   GUEST POST: ☐

PUBLICATION DATE:

TITLE:

CATEGORY:

KEYWORDS:

NOTES:

PUBLICATION DATE:

TITLE:

CATEGORY:

KEYWORDS:

NOTES:

PUBLICATION DATE:

TITLE:

CATEGORY:

KEYWORDS:

NOTES:

Post Planner

WEEK OF: _____

TYPE: ARTICLE: TUTORIAL: REVIEW: GUEST POST:

PUBLICATION DATE:

TITLE:

CATEGORY:

KEYWORDS:

NOTES:

PUBLICATION DATE:

TITLE:

CATEGORY:

KEYWORDS:

NOTES:

PUBLICATION DATE:

TITLE:

CATEGORY:

KEYWORDS:

NOTES:

Post Planner

WEEK OF: _____

TYPE: ARTICLE: ☐   TUTORIAL: ☐   REVIEW: ☐   GUEST POST: ☐

PUBLICATION DATE:

TITLE:

CATEGORY:

KEYWORDS:

NOTES:

LIST BUILDING PROGRESS:

SUBSCRIBERS: EMAILED THIS WEEK ✉

SOCIAL MEDIA PROMO THIS WEEK:

☐ 🐦   ☐ f   ☐ 𝓅   ☐ 📷   ☐ ▶   in   g+

EXTERNAL LINKS: PRODUCTS PROMOTED:

INTERNAL LINKS:

                                   Affiliate Disclaimer
                                   Included

Guest Post Planner

POST TITLE:

PUBLISH DATE: CATEGORY:

MAIN TOPIC:

POST SUMMARY:

KEY POINTS:

INCLUDED LINKS:

SHARED ON:

FACEBOOK   INSTAGRAM

TWITTER   PINTEREST

TAGS & KEYWORDS:

OF COMMENTS: # OF TRACKBACKS:

NOTES:

Marketing Planner

TOP TRAFFIC CHANNELS:

MARKETING TO DO LIST:

FREE ADVERTISING IDEAS:

PAID ADVERTISING IDEAS:

Marketing Tracker

PROMOTIONAL STRATEGIES TO MAXIMIZE EXPOSURE

PROMOTIONAL IDEAS:

MARKETING TO DO:

SOCIAL MEDIA GROWTH TRACKER:

	BEFORE:	AFTER:
f		
🐦		
📌		
▶		

OTHER:

LIST BUILDING & ENGAGEMENT:

MAILING LIST
SUBSCRIBERS:

OF EMAILS SENT
TO SUBSCRIBERS:

OF NEW BLOG
POSTS THIS WEEK:

OF COMPLETED
GUEST POSTS:

NOTES:

September

TASKS, MARKETING, ENGAGEMENT & MONETIZATION

CONTENT IDEAS

PROMOTION IDEAS

TOP PRIORITIES

MONTHLY FOCUS

MONETIZATION RESOURCES

Monthly Goals

MAIN OBJECTIVE:

GOAL:

ACTION STEPS:

GOAL:

ACTION STEPS:

GOAL:

ACTION STEPS:

TRAFFIC STATS:

MAILING LIST SUBSCRIBERS:

Content Planner

POST TITLE:

TARGETED KEYWORDS:

SOCIAL SHARING:

TOPIC OUTLINE:

PUBLICATION DATE:

TO DO CHECKLIST:

Research Topic

Pinpoint Target Audience

Choose target keywords

Optimize for search engines

Link to other blog post

Create post images

Proofread & Edit Post

Schedule Post Date

NOTES:

Content Planner

CATEGORY:

RESOURCE LINKS:

GRAPHICS/IMAGES:

KEY POINTS:

SEO CHECKLIST:

Primary keyword in post title

Secondary keyword in sub-title

Keyword in first paragraph

Word count > 1000 words

1-2 Outbound Links

Internal Link Structure

Post URL includes keywords

Meta description added

Post includes images

Post includes sub-headlines

Social sharing enabled

NOTES:

Post Planner

WEEK OF: _____

TYPE: ARTICLE: ☐   TUTORIAL: ☐   REVIEW: ☐   GUEST POST: ☐

PUBLICATION DATE:

TITLE:

CATEGORY:

KEYWORDS:

NOTES:

PUBLICATION DATE:

TITLE:

CATEGORY:

KEYWORDS:

NOTES:

PUBLICATION DATE:

TITLE:

CATEGORY:

KEYWORDS:

NOTES:

Post Planner

WEEK OF: _____

TYPE: ARTICLE: ☐   TUTORIAL: ☐   REVIEW: ☐   GUEST POST: ☐

PUBLICATION DATE:

TITLE:

CATEGORY:

KEYWORDS:

NOTES:

PUBLICATION DATE:

TITLE:

CATEGORY:

KEYWORDS:

NOTES:

PUBLICATION DATE:

TITLE:

CATEGORY:

KEYWORDS:

NOTES:

Post Planner

WEEK OF: _____

TYPE: ARTICLE: ☐   TUTORIAL: ☐   REVIEW: ☐   GUEST POST: ☐

PUBLICATION DATE:

TITLE:

CATEGORY:

KEYWORDS:

NOTES:

LIST BUILDING PROGRESS:

SUBSCRIBERS: _____   EMAILED THIS WEEK ✉

SOCIAL MEDIA PROMO THIS WEEK:

☐ 🐦   ☐ f   ☐ 𝓟   ☐ 📷   ☐ ▶   in   g+

EXTERNAL LINKS: PRODUCTS PROMOTED:

INTERNAL LINKS:

Affiliate Disclaimer
Included

Guest Post Planner

POST TITLE:

PUBLISH DATE: CATEGORY:

MAIN TOPIC:

POST SUMMARY:

KEY POINTS:

INCLUDED LINKS:

SHARED ON:

FACEBOOK   INSTAGRAM

TWITTER   PINTEREST

TAGS & KEYWORDS:

OF COMMENTS: # OF TRACKBACKS:

NOTES:

Marketing Planner

TOP TRAFFIC CHANNELS:

MARKETING TO DO LIST:

FREE ADVERTISING IDEAS:

PAID ADVERTISING IDEAS:

Marketing Tracker

PROMOTIONAL STRATEGIES TO MAXIMIZE EXPOSURE

PROMOTIONAL IDEAS:

MARKETING TO DO:

SOCIAL MEDIA GROWTH TRACKER:

BEFORE: AFTER:

f

⌗

🐦

P

▶

OTHER:

LIST BUILDING & ENGAGEMENT:

MAILING LIST
SUBSCRIBERS:

OF EMAILS SENT
TO SUBSCRIBERS:

OF NEW BLOG
POSTS THIS WEEK:

OF COMPLETED
GUEST POSTS:

NOTES:

October

TASKS, MARKETING, ENGAGEMENT & MONETIZATION

CONTENT IDEAS

PROMOTION IDEAS

TOP PRIORITIES

MONTHLY FOCUS

MONETIZATION RESOURCES

Monthly Goals

MAIN OBJECTIVE:

GOAL:

ACTION STEPS:

GOAL:

ACTION STEPS:

GOAL:

ACTION STEPS:

TRAFFIC STATS:

MAILING LIST SUBSCRIBERS:

Content Planner

POST TITLE:

PUBLICATION DATE:

TARGETED KEYWORDS:

TO DO CHECKLIST:

- Research Topic
- Pinpoint Target Audience
- Choose target keywords
- Optimize for search engines
- Link to other blog post
- Create post images
- Proofread & Edit Post
- Schedule Post Date

SOCIAL SHARING:

TOPIC OUTLINE:

NOTES:

Content Planner

CATEGORY:

RESOURCE LINKS:

GRAPHICS/IMAGES:

KEY POINTS:

SEO CHECKLIST:

Primary keyword in post title

Secondary keyword in sub-title

Keyword in first paragraph

Word count > 1000 words

1-2 Outbound Links

Internal Link Structure

Post URL includes keywords

Meta description added

Post includes images

Post includes sub-headlines

Social sharing enabled

NOTES:

Post Planner

WEEK OF: _____

TYPE: ARTICLE: ☐   TUTORIAL: ☐   REVIEW: ☐   GUEST POST: ☐

PUBLICATION DATE:

TITLE:

CATEGORY:

KEYWORDS:

NOTES:

PUBLICATION DATE:

TITLE:

CATEGORY:

KEYWORDS:

NOTES:

PUBLICATION DATE:

TITLE:

CATEGORY:

KEYWORDS:

NOTES:

Post Planner

WEEK OF: _____

TYPE: ARTICLE: TUTORIAL: REVIEW: GUEST POST:

PUBLICATION DATE:

TITLE:

CATEGORY:

KEYWORDS:

NOTES:

PUBLICATION DATE:

TITLE:

CATEGORY:

KEYWORDS:

NOTES:

PUBLICATION DATE:

TITLE:

CATEGORY:

KEYWORDS:

NOTES:

Post Planner

WEEK OF: _____

TYPE: ARTICLE: TUTORIAL: REVIEW: GUEST POST:

PUBLICATION DATE:

TITLE:

CATEGORY:

KEYWORDS:

NOTES:

LIST BUILDING PROGRESS:

SUBSCRIBERS: EMAILED THIS WEEK

SOCIAL MEDIA PROMO THIS WEEK:

EXTERNAL LINKS: PRODUCTS PROMOTED:

INTERNAL LINKS:

Affiliate Disclaimer
Included

Guest Post Planner

POST TITLE:

PUBLISH DATE: CATEGORY:

MAIN TOPIC:

POST SUMMARY:

KEY POINTS:

INCLUDED LINKS:

SHARED ON: FACEBOOK   INSTAGRAM

             TWITTER   PINTEREST

TAGS & KEYWORDS: # OF COMMENTS: # OF TRACKBACKS:

                        NOTES:

Marketing Planner

TOP TRAFFIC CHANNELS:

MARKETING TO DO LIST:

FREE ADVERTISING IDEAS:

PAID ADVERTISING IDEAS:

Marketing Tracker

PROMOTIONAL STRATEGIES TO MAXIMIZE EXPOSURE

PROMOTIONAL IDEAS:

MARKETING TO DO:

SOCIAL MEDIA GROWTH TRACKER:

BEFORE: AFTER:

OTHER:

LIST BUILDING & ENGAGEMENT:

MAILING LIST
SUBSCRIBERS:

OF EMAILS SENT
TO SUBSCRIBERS:

OF NEW BLOG
POSTS THIS WEEK:

OF COMPLETED
GUEST POSTS:

NOTES:

November

TASKS, MARKETING, ENGAGEMENT & MONETIZATION

CONTENT IDEAS

PROMOTION IDEAS

TOP PRIORITIES

MONTHLY FOCUS

MONETIZATION RESOURCES

Monthly Goals

MAIN OBJECTIVE:

GOAL:

ACTION STEPS:

GOAL:

ACTION STEPS:

GOAL:

ACTION STEPS:

TRAFFIC STATS:

MAILING LIST SUBSCRIBERS:

Content Planner

POST TITLE:

PUBLICATION DATE:

TARGETED KEYWORDS:

TO DO CHECKLIST:

    Research Topic

    Pinpoint Target Audience

    Choose target keywords

    Optimize for search engines

    Link to other blog post

    Create post images

    Proofread & Edit Post

    Schedule Post Date

SOCIAL SHARING: (circle all that apply)

TOPIC OUTLINE:

NOTES:

Content Planner

CATEGORY:

RESOURCE LINKS:

GRAPHICS/IMAGES:

KEY POINTS:

SEO CHECKLIST:

Primary keyword in post title

Secondary keyword in sub-title

Keyword in first paragraph

Word count > 1000 words

1-2 Outbound Links

Internal Link Structure

Post URL includes keywords

Meta description added

Post includes images

Post includes sub-headlines

Social sharing enabled

NOTES:

Post Planner

WEEK OF: _____

TYPE: ARTICLE: ☐   TUTORIAL: ☐   REVIEW: ☐   GUEST POST: ☐

PUBLICATION DATE:

TITLE:

CATEGORY:

KEYWORDS:

NOTES:

PUBLICATION DATE:

TITLE:

CATEGORY:

KEYWORDS:

NOTES:

PUBLICATION DATE:

TITLE:

CATEGORY:

KEYWORDS:

NOTES:

Post Planner

WEEK OF: _____

TYPE: ARTICLE: ☐   TUTORIAL: ☐   REVIEW: ☐   GUEST POST: ☐

PUBLICATION DATE:

TITLE:

CATEGORY:

KEYWORDS:

NOTES:

PUBLICATION DATE:

TITLE:

CATEGORY:

KEYWORDS:

NOTES:

PUBLICATION DATE:

TITLE:

CATEGORY:

KEYWORDS:

NOTES:

Post Planner

WEEK OF: _____

TYPE: ARTICLE: ☐   TUTORIAL: ☐   REVIEW: ☐   GUEST POST: ☐

PUBLICATION DATE:

TITLE:

CATEGORY:

KEYWORDS:

NOTES:

LIST BUILDING PROGRESS:

SUBSCRIBERS: EMAILED THIS WEEK ✉

SOCIAL MEDIA PROMO THIS WEEK:

☐ 🐦   ☐ f   ☐ 𝓟   ☐ 📷   ☐ ▶   ☐ in   ☐ g+

EXTERNAL LINKS: PRODUCTS PROMOTED:

INTERNAL LINKS:

Affiliate Disclaimer
Included

Guest Post Planner

POST TITLE:

PUBLISH DATE: CATEGORY:

MAIN TOPIC:

POST SUMMARY:

KEY POINTS:

INCLUDED LINKS:

SHARED ON:
- FACEBOOK
- TWITTER
- INSTAGRAM
- PINTEREST

TAGS & KEYWORDS:

OF COMMENTS: # OF TRACKBACKS:

NOTES:

Marketing Planner

TOP TRAFFIC CHANNELS:

MARKETING TO DO LIST:

FREE ADVERTISING IDEAS:

PAID ADVERTISING IDEAS:

Marketing Tracker

PROMOTIONAL STRATEGIES TO MAXIMIZE EXPOSURE

PROMOTIONAL IDEAS:

MARKETING TO DO:

SOCIAL MEDIA GROWTH TRACKER:

	BEFORE:	AFTER:

OTHER:

LIST BUILDING & ENGAGEMENT:

MAILING LIST
SUBSCRIBERS:

OF EMAILS SENT
TO SUBSCRIBERS:

OF NEW BLOG
POSTS THIS WEEK:

OF COMPLETED
GUEST POSTS:

NOTES:

December

TASKS, MARKETING, ENGAGEMENT & MONETIZATION

CONTENT IDEAS

PROMOTION IDEAS

TOP PRIORITIES

MONTHLY FOCUS

MONETIZATION RESOURCES

Monthly Goals

MAIN OBJECTIVE:

GOAL:

ACTION STEPS:

GOAL:

ACTION STEPS:

GOAL:

ACTION STEPS:

TRAFFIC STATS:

MAILING LIST SUBSCRIBERS:

Content Planner

POST TITLE:

PUBLICATION DATE:

TARGETED KEYWORDS:

TO DO CHECKLIST:

- Research Topic
- Pinpoint Target Audience
- Choose target keywords
- Optimize for search engines
- Link to other blog post
- Create post images
- Proofread & Edit Post
- Schedule Post Date

SOCIAL SHARING:

NOTES:

TOPIC OUTLINE:

Content Planner

CATEGORY:

RESOURCE LINKS:

GRAPHICS/IMAGES:

KEY POINTS:

SEO CHECKLIST:

Primary keyword in post title

Secondary keyword in sub-title

Keyword in first paragraph

Word count > 1000 words

1-2 Outbound Links

Internal Link Structure

Post URL includes keywords

Meta description added

Post includes images

Post includes sub-headlines

Social sharing enabled

NOTES:

Post Planner

WEEK OF: _____

TYPE: ARTICLE: ⬜ TUTORIAL: ⬜ REVIEW: ⬜ GUEST POST: ⬜

PUBLICATION DATE:

TITLE:

CATEGORY:

KEYWORDS:

NOTES:

PUBLICATION DATE:

TITLE:

CATEGORY:

KEYWORDS:

NOTES:

PUBLICATION DATE:

TITLE:

CATEGORY:

KEYWORDS:

NOTES:

Post Planner

WEEK OF: _____

TYPE: ARTICLE: TUTORIAL: REVIEW: GUEST POST:

PUBLICATION DATE:

TITLE:

CATEGORY:

KEYWORDS:

NOTES:

PUBLICATION DATE:

TITLE:

CATEGORY:

KEYWORDS:

NOTES:

PUBLICATION DATE:

TITLE:

CATEGORY:

KEYWORDS:

NOTES:

Post Planner

WEEK OF: _____

TYPE: ARTICLE: ☐ TUTORIAL: ☐ REVIEW: ☐ GUEST POST: ☐

PUBLICATION DATE:

TITLE:

CATEGORY:

KEYWORDS:

NOTES:

LIST BUILDING PROGRESS:

SUBSCRIBERS: EMAILED THIS WEEK ✉

SOCIAL MEDIA PROMO THIS WEEK:

☐ 🐦 ☐ f ☐ 𝓟 ☐ 📷 ☐ ▶ in g+

EXTERNAL LINKS: PRODUCTS PROMOTED:

INTERNAL LINKS:

Affiliate Disclaimer
Included

Guest Post Planner

POST TITLE:

PUBLISH DATE: CATEGORY:

MAIN TOPIC:

POST SUMMARY:

KEY POINTS:

INCLUDED LINKS:

SHARED ON:

FACEBOOK   INSTAGRAM

TWITTER   PINTEREST

TAGS & KEYWORDS:

OF COMMENTS: # OF TRACKBACKS:

NOTES:

Marketing Planner

TOP TRAFFIC CHANNELS:

MARKETING TO DO LIST:

FREE ADVERTISING IDEAS:

PAID ADVERTISING IDEAS:

Marketing Tracker

PROMOTIONAL STRATEGIES TO MAXIMIZE EXPOSURE

PROMOTIONAL IDEAS:

MARKETING TO DO:

SOCIAL MEDIA GROWTH TRACKER:

	BEFORE:	AFTER:
f		
Instagram		
Twitter		
Pinterest		
YouTube		

OTHER:

LIST BUILDING & ENGAGEMENT:

MAILING LIST
SUBSCRIBERS:

OF EMAILS SENT
TO SUBSCRIBERS:

OF NEW BLOG
POSTS THIS WEEK:

OF COMPLETED
GUEST POSTS:

NOTES:

Bonus Page

CREATE YOUR OWN CHECKLISTS!

NOTES:

Bonus Page

CREATE YOUR OWN CHECKLISTS!

NOTES:

www.ingramcontent.com/pod-product-compliance
Lightning Source LLC
Chambersburg PA
CBHW080537060326
40690CB00022B/5151